Consider Love

To: Ty lee

From: TPS

DEDICATED

To

James Patrick George Jawbone McEwan

Published by Simon & Schuster, 1230 Avenue of the Americas, New York, New York 10020
©2002 Sandra Boynton. All rights reserved, including the right of reproduction in whole or in part in any form.
Printed in the United States of America
First Edition
2 4 6 8 10 9 7 5 3 1
Library of Congress Cataloging-in-Publication Data
Boynton, Sandra
Consider Love : its moods and many ways / written and illustrated by Sandra Boynton
p. cm.   ISBN 0-689-84703-3
1. Love poetry, American. I. Title.   PS3552.O947 C6 2002   811'.54--dc21   2001034480

CONSIDER LOVE

Its Moods and Many Ways

written and illustrated by

Sandra Boynton

Simon & Schuster

New York London Toronto Sydney Singapore

Consider love.
Look here and there.
Consider love.
It's everywhere.
Consider love.
Observe a while.
It comes in every
shape, and style.

Szindis Zarnier
(1891–1988)
CONSIDER LOVE
oil on canvas
1937

5

There's simple love

and love
mysterious.

Frivolous
love

and love
too serious.

There's hopeful love

and love despairing.

Cautious love

and love that's daring.

There's
tiny love

and love
unbounded.

Logical love

and love unfounded.

Love that's shallow.

Love
that's
deep.

Love  extravagant.

Love...
well, cheap.

Love that is clever.

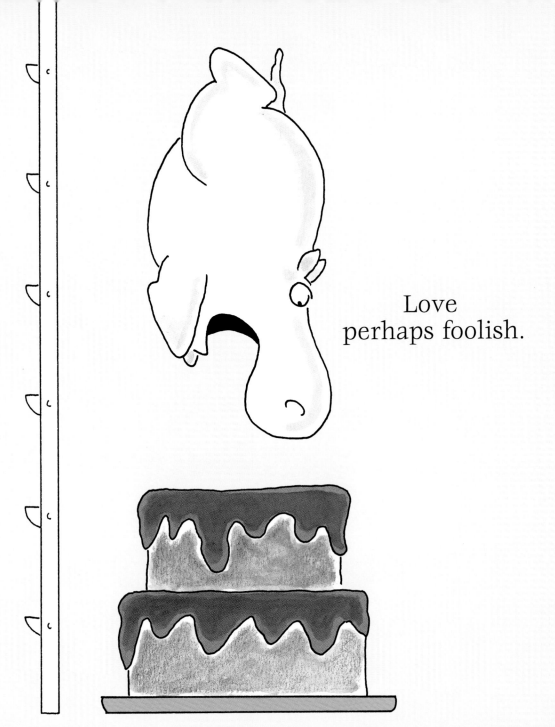

Love
perhaps foolish.

Love oh so hot.

Love rather coolish.

Young love.

Old love.

Meek love.

Bold love.

Eloquent love

and
never-told
love.

Love that's inspiring.

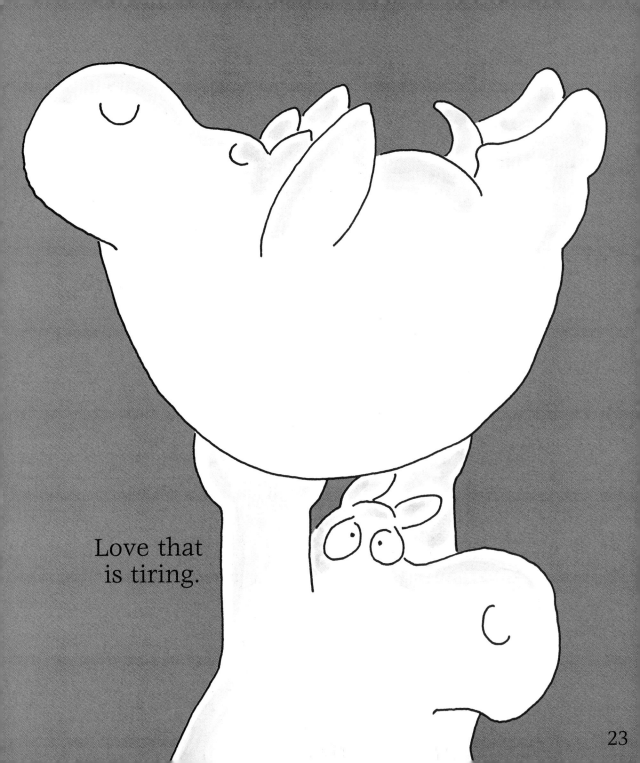

Love that
is tiring.

23

Love over-jealous.

Comfortable love

and love problematic.

Love
wistful and weary.

Love gently ecstatic.

Theatrical love
that can
suffer

or smile,

make grand declarations,

and exit with style.

Now consider
one love
in the
midst of
the crowd—

an affectionate love,
neither timid nor loud.
A love that appreciates
fire, and grace.
A love that adores
one remarkable face.
A love that is
steady,
devoted,
and true—

Consider my love for incredible you.